The Complete Guide to Digital, Smart Phone & Online Couponing

by
Aaron Publishing

Aaron Publishing
PO Box 1144
Shelbyville, TN 37162
www.aaronpublishing.com

The Complete Guide to Digital, Smart Phone & Online Couponing
Copyright © 2013 by Aaron Publishing

First Printing 2013

Aaron Publishing
PO Box 1144
Shelbyville, TN 37162
www.aaronpublishing.com

The Complete Guide to Digital, Smart Phone
&
Online Couponing

Table of Contents

1

The Wide World of Web Couponing

It is no surprise that couponing has teamed up with modern technology and become a resource we can now find without ever leaving the comforts of our home via the internet. It is estimated that only 2% of Americans cannot get internet access and only 20% choose not to take part in internet usage. [1] This tells us the vast majority of people do in fact use the internet. Manufacturers realize their opportunity to increase coupon usage must include the world wide web.

Many however, are still unsure of how to use online, digital and even smart phone coupons to their advantage. Others simply don't want to take the time to learn this new skill and join the millions of people who are saving as a result of them.

In this manual I will uncover some of the basic questions the consumer asks in regard to using the internet as a resource for saving money. Many will decide to take advantage of this, while others will remain in the comfort zone of Sunday paper clipping to provide most of their savings. No matter which category you fall into it is always a good idea to learn how to use the resource even if you do not consistently use it. I always say "knowledge is never wasted." Keeping on top of the changing times gives consumers an edge to understanding the economy and enables them to make wise financial decisions.

Analysts believe the online coupon market will reach 104.9 million by 2015. This would be an increase of 14% since 2012. Smart phone coupon usage will also increase 32% from 40.8 million in 2012. [2]

So what are the key factors driving this usage up? Let's take a look at some elements that contribute to this new advancement in technology:

[1] http://www.theverge.com/2013/8/26/4660008/pew-study-finds-30-percent-americans-have-no-home-broadband
[2] http://www.bloomberg.com/news/2013-08-22/retailmenot-sales-beat-analyst-estimates-as-coupon-use-climbs.html

#1 Most Americans have access to a computer even if their local newspaper does not have weekly coupon inserts.

#2 Most all consumers own a phone and with the price of smart phones dropping as technology advances many are switching over to smart phones.

#3 Consumers always have a coupon in hand with their phone even when they forget and leave the clipped coupons on the kitchen table.

#4 Consumers are able to search & find the coupon they want on a as needed basis

#5 Many prefer online shopping as opposed to hitting the stores.

#6 Online couponing keeps print & advertising costs down.

All of these factors contribute largely to the increase we see in online coupon availability. The roll of the consumer must now be to understand the types of coupons presented through modern day technology as well how to maximize on their benefits without becoming a computer crazed couponer.

One of the largest disadvantages I see and have experienced myself is online couponing can be time consuming as we browse site after site often duplicating the same available coupons. On the other hand, one of the greatest advantages I see and have experienced myself is the availability of the coupon you want and need, thus limiting overspending by buying unwanted products.

An article in yahoo finance recently reported one of the top 28 ways consumers waste money is with couponing.[1] What they referred to is the many consumers who will make purchases they normally wouldn't just because a coupon presented itself. This brings us to a very important fact and probably the key to all successful couponing endeavors:

[1]http://finance.yahoo.com/news/ways-waste-money-slide-show-040001799.html?page=all

You control the coupon, don't let it control you!

A wise shopper will be quick to understand that with increased technology comes increased marketing tactics meant to cause the consumer to spend unnecessary money. I find it quite amusing that when the coupon show appeared on television extreme couponers boasted of their phenomenal savings showing off their newly added addition to their house to house all their savings. Here's a question for consideration: If you must build an addition on to your house to stock your savings did you really save any money?

Don't get me wrong couponing is great way to save money and in all honesty the very resource that kept my family self-sufficient instead of government dependent during my husband's job layoffs. We were able to save $800 a month with this amazing resource and now have even increased that with the internet coupon availability. Just be wise, don't make quick decisions without understanding the principles that surround the usage and never buy what you won't use or don't need. If you have one dollar left, the place to put it is in the savings account not on the amazing dollar deal to good to pass up.

In the next several chapters we are going to take a look at types of digital couponing including ecoupons, smart phone coupons, printable coupons and even coupon coded coupons for online purchases. You will learn what they are, what their purpose is, where to find them, how to use them, when to avoid them and more.

If you're ready to dive in to the wide world of web couponing turn to chapter 2 and let's get started.

Happy Hunting.....The Future Starts Here!

2

Printable Coupons

Let's take a look at what is known as the "Coupon Database." This is simply a site where current coupons are listed from all sources-Sunday supplements, blinkies, tearpads, home mailers, etc., as well as printable coupons. Simply stated sites you can search for coupons based upon your specific needs which are currently available. The internet is covered up with these sites, some are more user friendly than others and based upon your particular deciphering ability some will be easier to navigate than others. The key is to locate a site that simplifies your search by appealing to your ability. Not everyone will benefit from all sites, but there are some that rank among the top with most couponers. We will look at some of these but, before we do let's understand there are two types of coupons you will be searching for and different sites mean different deals:

"Those for grocery (edible) items"
&
"Those for material (non edible) items"

Now let's take a look at two well-known sites for great finds: (It's important to mention that most blog sites do have coupon databases you can access for ease in your search as well)

www.afullcup.com
www.coupontom.com

On the next page we want to look at a sample from one of these sites to understand how to maneuver it to find your specific coupon. Unless you understand what you're looking at you'll never be able to find what you're looking for. The best thing about these sites is it stops the endless search for a coupon that doesn't exist, therefore saving you endless hours of frustration.

NOTE: You will have to register on all sites before you can have access to print the coupons you desire.

Navigating a coupon database[1]:

Description	Value	Coupon Type	Category	Store	Expired
		All ▼	All ▼	All ▼	Hide Expired ▼

Reset   Submit

0-9 A B C D E F G H I J K L M N O P Q R S T U V W X Y Z

The first thing you will generally notice is the description. Here is where you will key in specifically what you are looking for. For example:

Description	Value	Coupon Type	Category	Store	Expired
pizza		All ▼	All ▼	All ▼	Hide Expired ▼

Reset   Submit

0-9 A B C D E F G H I J K L M N O P Q R S T U V W X Y Z

Note: The alphabet above will allow you to look for everything starting with that particular letter. If I had clicked on "p" it would have brought up every available coupon starting with the letter "p."

Description	Value	Coupon Type	Category	Store	Expire
pizza	$1	All ▼	All ▼	All ▼	Hide

Reset

0-9 A B C D E F G H I J K L M N O P Q R S T U V W X Y Z

Description	Value	Expires	Coupon Type	Category	Select
DiGiorno pizza dipping strips	$1.00/1	Rolling	Printable	Frozen – Other	☐
DiGiorno small pizzas	$1.00/2	09/30/2013	Sunday Supplement 08/25/2013 RP	Frozen	☐
Don Pepino pizza sauce	$1.00/3	Rolling	Printable	Grocery – Canned Other	☐
Ellio's Pizza Varieties	$1.00/2	09/30/2013	Printable	Grocery	☐
FIVE Totino's Crisp Crust Party Pizza	$1.00/1	09/30/2013	Printable	Frozen – Meats	☐
lia.com... Crust Party Pizza	$1.00/1	10/30/2013	Printable	Frozen – Meats	☐

Type in coupon type, ex. printable, blinkie, tearpad, etc...

Description	Value	Coupon Type	Category	Store	Expi
pizza	$1	Printable ▼	All ▼	All ▼	Hic

Reset

0-9 A B C D E F G H I J K L M N O P Q R S T U V W X Y Z

Description	Value	Expires	Coupon Type	Category	Select
DiGiorno pizza dipping strips	$1.00/1	Rolling	Printable	Frozen – Other	☐
Don Pepino pizza sauce	$1.00/3	Rolling	Printable	Grocery – Canned Other	☐
Ellio's Pizza Varieties	$1.00/2	09/30/2013	Printable	Grocery	☐
FIVE Totino's Crisp Crust Party Pizza	$1.00/1	09/30/2013	Printable	Frozen – Meats	☐

Here you can type in specific categories, ex. restaurant, frozen, etc.

Description	Value	Coupon Type	Category	Store	Expired
pizza	$1	Printable ▼	Frozen ▼	All ▼	Hide Exp

Reset

0-9 A B C D E F G H I J K L M N O P Q R S T U V W X Y Z

Description	Value	Expires	Coupon Type	Category	Select
Freschetta pizza, 14 oz – no more prints	$1.00/1	Rolling	Printable	Frozen	☐

Looking for a specific store choose from the drop down box here:

Description	Value	Coupon Type	Category	Store	Expire
cheese		All ▼	All ▼	Publix ▼	Hide

Reset

0-9 A B C D E F G H I J K L M N O P Q R S T U V W X Y Z

Description	Value	Expires	Coupon Type	Category	Select
Friendship Cottage Cheese Product	$0.55/1	03/31/2020	Booklet/Pamphlet	Dairy – Cheese	☐

Printing from a coupon database:

Select the coupon you wish to print. Then click print coupon.

Description	Value	Coupon Type	Category	Store	Expired
kraft cheese		All ▾	All ▾	All ▾	Hide Expired ▾

Reset   Submit

0-9 A B C D E F G H I J K L M N O P Q R S T U V W X Y Z

Description	Value	Expires	Coupon Type	Category	Select
(2) KRAFT or CRACKER BARREL Cheese	$1.50/1	10/14/2013	Printable	Dairy – Cheese	✓

🖨 Print Coupons

Next mark "clip" and click the print button.

Before you will be issued rights to print a coupon you must first install the "coupon driver." Once you click on print coupons it will alert you to install the driver. It might look like this:

Coupon Printer
for Windows
click here to download

Coupon Printer
for Macintosh
click here to download

[Supported on Internet Explorer, Firefox, Chrome, Safari, Opera & Netscape]

[Supported on Safari, Firefox & Chrome]

Click "Save File." Once you install the printer you will not need to do it each time you want to print a coupon. The coupon printer is a

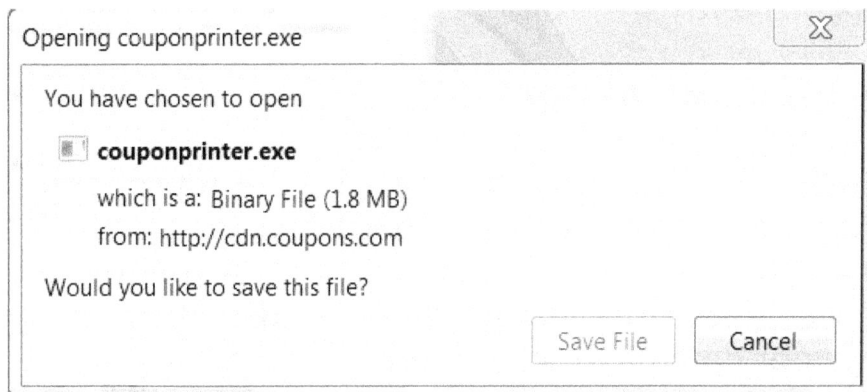

trusted download powered by TRUSTe privacy. For more information on what platforms are supported by this printer go to:

http://www.coupons.com/couponweb/help/print/install.html

Troubleshooting Coupon Printing:

Most websites require you to install coupon printing software. This free software download enables your printer to print barcodes. If the coupon printer doesn't install, you may need to adjust security levels to allow ActiveX items – (like the coupon printer) to install. If you are using Windows XP, SP2, or Vista, a yellow information bar should appear at the top of your window. That bar can only appear if your security levels are set to "medium" and all ActiveX items are set to "prompt" or "enable." The yellow bar may ask you for permission to download content before installation starts. In that case, follow the instructions to allow the download.

You may have had a problem in the past with another download that has disabled the prompt for downloads. If so, you can try downloading a new browser to give your browser a fresh start. If you have Internet Explorer you can try downloading firefox. (www.mozilla.com/firefox.com)

Just knowing which browser you use is a great start! A browser is the progam you use to open internet pages such as: Internet Explorer, FireFox or Safari.

Which browser are you using:

Click "Help" on your toolbar menu at the top of the screen. One of the options should be "About Mozilla Firefox," "About Internet Explorer," or "About Safari." Select this option and a window will open that displays the name, version number, and copyright date of your browser.

Or look at the very top of the computer screen right above the area that you type a web address to see what browser is displayed.

If after clicking a link to print a coupon you get "Please wait"....and you wait and nothing happens, or "Please Install The Coupon Printer" even if you already have, or "You have already printed this coupon" and you know you haven't... you are not alone and there's really not much you can do at that point.

If a coupon link is created in FireFox, and you have Internet Explorer or Safari, they don't work together. In other words, the browser that your computer uses and the link that you click to print have to both use the same browser or it won't work. For example, if you use Internet Explorer and the link that you click was created in Safari – they won't work together and vice versa.

Summarizing it all:

The following is a FireFox link:

http://bricks.coupons.com/
Start.aspt59687503&bt=wg&o=53740&ci=1&cJAY#sthash.ccI1bZG
3.dpuf

Note the "wg" in the URL. If your browser is Internet Explorer you will continue to get the message "Please Install The Coupon

Printer." To change the link to work on an Internet Explorer link simply change "wg" to "wi" or "vi." Most of the time either will work, however there may a coupon that works on one and not the other. ("wi" or "vi") In that case it's trial and error.

http://bricks.coupons.com/
Start.asp59687503&bt=wi&o=53740&ci=1&cJAY

Or

http://bricks.coupons.com/
Start.asp59687503&bt=vi&o=53740&ci=1&cJAY

In a Nutshell, find out what browser your computer is operating on. When you have trouble printing check the letters in the URL. If the letters don't correspond with the browser you are using, then change the two magical characters to match your browser. Below is the list of browsers along with their matchups:

Firefox = "wg" or "vg"
Internet Explore = "wi" or "vi"
Safari = "xs" [1]

Identifying legitimate printable coupons:

All printable coupons should contain specific information for legitimacy. If you are ever in doubt Google search the coupon on coupon blog sites. Most coupon bloggers are up to date on fraudulent coupons that might be floating around. The key is:

"If it sounds to good to be true, it probably is."

[1]*http://www.time2saveworkshops.com/solutions-for-printing-problems/*

Here is an example of a printable coupon and what should be identifiable on it:

| 1 | TARGET WEB COUPON | 2 EXPIRES 9/1/07 |

3 **Complimentary**
Starbucks Grande size
prepared beverage
with beverage purchase of
same size

5
Limit one coupon per guest, one item
or offer per coupon. Void if copied,
transferred, purchased, sold or prohibited
by law. No cash value. Offer good while
quantities last. Maximum retail value 5.70
for free item.

4

6

9856-0113-9294-1115-1224-4724-47

1. Type of coupon should be identified (Store or Manufacturer)
2. Expiration date should be visible
3. Item offered or discount should be the main feature
4. Barcode should be on the face of coupon
5. Coupon rules should be listed (usually on lower corner)
6. If the coupon is a store coupon it will usually have the store logo, if not it will contain an address on where to mail the coupon for reimbursement from the manufacturer

Top most popular coupon sites for saving money:

Retailmenot.com
Groupon.com
Livingsocial.com
Coupons.com
Slickdeals.com
Smartsource.com
Fatwallet.com
Dealfind.com
Coolsavings.com

Top most popular sites for earning money while saving:

Upromise.com
eBates.com
Swagbucks.com
Shopathome.com
Mrrebates.com

    The way these sites work is by allowing you to shop from thousands of well-known stores through their site and earn a percentage of your purchase back. Most of them will have a minimum amount that you must earn before they will issue you a check or deposit it in your Paypal account. (Usually the minimum amount is around $5) Once you register on their site, you simply click on the store you wish to shop at, make your purchase and your account will show the percentage you earned. This is a great way to earn money while saving money. Use discount codes in conjunction with these sites to reduce the cost of the item. For example, some may offer free shipping, 20% off, buy one get one 50% off, etc...

3

Digital Coupons

Digital coupons are often referred to as "eCoupons." What is an eCoupon, you may be wondering? An eCoupon is simply this:

"An eCoupon is a clip-free coupon that is found on the internet offering a discount on a particular item at a particular store."

Many people prefer the eCoupon over the in-hand coupon because you don't leave it at home and it proves more effortless than cutting coupons. It is important to understand some of the basics rules when using the eCoupon as opposed to the in-hand paper coupon. Here they are:

1. eCoupons don't double (whereas paper coupons often do at participating stores up to a certain amount.)
2. They cannot be stacked with manufacturer coupon because they are manufacturer coupons
3. They cannot be stacked with a store coupon (varies by store, check your store for specifics)
4. eCoupons are loaded to your loyalty shopper card or attached to your phone number by choosing them online
5. Some limits apply to the number that can be loaded to your loyalty card or phone number (these vary by type and store)
6. eCoupons will come off your loyalty card or phone number once they have expired or have been used without you manually doing it
7. eCoupons may only be used for 1 discount even when purchasing 2 of the same item

You can check with your local store to see if they offer eCoupons directly through their store by emailing them or searching on their website. Some of the most popular eCoupon sites are:

Cellfire.com
Pgsaver.com
Krogers.com
Publix.com
Upromise.com
Shortcuts.com

You will need to register on each site you choose to get coupons from. Once you locate the coupon you wish to use simply click load card. The next step is go to the store and purchase the item for which you loaded on your card. Have the cashier scan the item and your card (or enter your phone number if the store does not have a loyalty card) and discount will automatically come off your purchase. Let's look at an example:

NOTE: Some sites offer eCoupons where the money is not actually deducted from your purchase, but rather deposited in an account for you to receive as a monetary payment. Some of these sites are:

Ibotta.com
Savingstar.com

How can you remember what coupons you clipped? Most sites will have an option for you to print a shopping list to keep track of these. See the example on the previous page on the green link. It is always a good idea to keep this print out in your coupon binder system to refer to when making out your grocery list.

A frequent question regarding eCoupons is this— "What do I do if my coupon discount does not come off my item?" Most sites have a customer service phone number you can call to request your refund. The refund is usually loaded back onto your loyalty shopper card and automatically deducts next time you make a purchase. On some occasions it doesn't hurt to mention it to the cashier; many times they will go ahead and manually give you the discount. You will know you got the discount when it shows up on your receipt as "eSavings or eCoupon."

All that is usually required to get your reimbursement is the transaction # from your receipt and your phone number. This is a fairly easy process and is usually worth the two minutes it takes to do it.

Here are two of the main customer service #'s for requesting reimbursements:

Publix— 866-486-4292 M-F 8-9 or email publixsupport@inmar.com

Krogers—888-553-3003 M-F 8-9

For more information regarding your specific store email them directly or inquire at customer service. Most stores have a specific department that deals with these type of situations.

These are a few of the major chain stores that participate in the eCoupon program:

Publix
Krogers
Winn Dixie
Bi-Lo
Food Lion
Safeway
Harris Teeter
& More..

You have probably become quite familiar with seeing this next little symbol around. It is a QR code which stands for "Quick Response Code." It is a trademark of a type of barcode known as a matrix barcode and is popular due to it's quicker readability.

The barcode is an optically machine-readable label that is attached to an item and that records information related to that item. It is the newest in technology, called the QR code. Many stores now display this scanable code which will then take you to the stores website and allow you special discounts related to their store.

Add them to any print advertising, flyers, posters, invites, TV ads etc containing:

- Product details
- Contact details
- Offer details
- Event details
- Competition details
- A coupon
- Twitter, Facebook, MySpace IDs
- A link to your YouTube video

4

Smart Phone Coupons

This will be by far my favorite chapter to tell you about. Smart phones are making their way into almost every household from the young to old. It is nothing to see a ten year old with an iPhone or Android sitting next to grandma, who is playing Angry Birds on hers. It won't be long till the basic phone is completely done away with and Smart Phones have replaced the market. Smart Phones have truly revolutionized the way we do business & conduct our social lives. Everything from planning your agenda on your calendar, tip figuring at the restaurant, making out your shopping list to having the cashier scan your phone for that extra discount on your new outfit.

In this chapter I want to talk about how the Smart Phone has revolutionized the way we save money by using the numerous savings apps they have made available. My phone is my best friend when it comes to shopping. It is nothing for me to pull out my phone in the mall, again at lunch and at the office store on the way home just to save a few more dollars. Does it really add up? Absolutely and the best part of all is the wide variety of stores that are jumping on board and participating in this new savings feature.

Before I tell you about some of the great apps that supply the biggest and best deals, I want to tell you how they work.

STEP1:

Go to your app store on your phone

Ex. Look for this symbol on your iPhone
Or
Look for this symbol on your Android
Or
Look for this symbol on your Windows

STEP 2:

Search "Free Coupon Apps"

STEP 3:

Locate the app you wish to download & click "free" then click "install app"

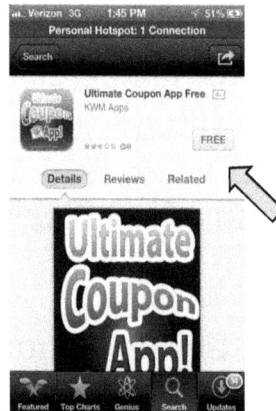

THAT'S ALL THERE IS TO IT! You are now ready to start using your new coupon app at thousands of major retailers. Remember it is not necessary to pay for an app unless it's one you really want. There are many amazing apps that you can get free of charge that will save you hundreds of dollars. Shopping just got easier. It's as simple as pulling up your app on your phone, searching for the store of your choice and checking availability of a coupon for your purchase. If a coupon is available it will appear on your phone. Now show it to the cashier and they will either scan it or enter the code on the coupon. I have literally saved hundreds of dollars using this method in almost every store I shop.

Let's look at an example:

(Here is a sample of how a coupon app might work—this one is taken from the Coupon Sherpa app)

Ex. #1—

Coupon App with a Barcode

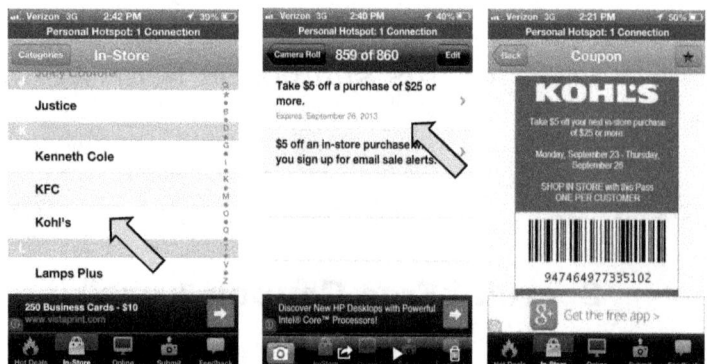

Ex. #2—

Coupon App without a Barcode

(the cashier will enter the code)

These apps can especially be great when you leave a coupon at home that a retailer had mailed you. Many times a wider variety will exist on these apps than the ones offered via mail. Restaurant apps are especially great for saving you money. These can also be accessed the same way the retail stores are found.

It is important to note that not all smart phone apps are scanable or can be entered by a code. Some require you to sign up through email, others require you print them out. In some instances stores may go ahead and give you the discount even if you did not print out the coupon if you show them the discount on your phone. I always say, "you won't know if you don't ask." This has paid off for me many times. Look at the samples below:

Some of the top smart phone apps are:

Coupon Sherpa (iPhone)
Yowza (iPhone)
Coupsmart (iPhone)
The Coupon App (Android & iPhone)
Coupons.com (Android & iPhone)
Snipsnap (iPhone &Android)
Cuckoo for Coupon Deals (Android)

Note: Even if you don't find the app you want for your specific smart phone, keep checking as technology is constantly changing and releasing new availability.

Some of the top sale search apps are:

Dealnews (Android & iPhone)
Shopsavy (Android, iPhone & Windows)
Decide.com (iPhone)
Amazon (iPhone & Android)

Fun apps for the couponer:

Fast Mall (navigate the mall including restrooms)
Shopkick (iPhone & Android)

Grocery List Making apps:

Grocery IQ
(this is the best Free app available, although there are others you can pay for)

In the last chapter I mentioned two apps that not only correlate with what you buy at the grocery store, but that make you money which can be deposited into a Paypal account after a minimum amount is saved. These two apps deserve taking a closer look at:

iBotta (Android & iPhone)
Saving Star (Android & iPhone)

The one I want to focus on has made a powerful name for itself, iBotta. It has been featured on Good Morning America and been in numerous news stories. Consumers are racking up the savings with this great app, some making thousands of dollars. I don't know about you, but a thousand extra dollars in my Christmas Club account would really come in handy. iBotta is a free app.

Some of the benefits of using iBotta are:

*Make money by buying products you use everyday

*Find great recipes, time saving tips, nutrition facts

*You determine what you earn by the tasks you choose to complete (less time consuming than cutting a coupon in many cases)

Here is how iBotta works:

*Sign up for the App on your Android or Apple device here : https://ibotta.com/r/88rwmg

*Browse the offers for the products you buy

*Complete the assigned task to redeem the savings amount desired

*Purchase the product at the participating store listed (if store is not listed contact them directly about adding this App)

*Use the App savings in conjunction with coupons for the best amount of savings (only one $$ reward will be given per item through the Ibotta App, however, using coupons in conjunction can lower your out of pocket expense and increase your profit margin after receiving your Ibotta refund bonus.)

*Upload the receipt in entirety (until all stores go receiptless)

*Scan the barcode of the item you purchased

*Collect your money via Paypal

*Upload any updates on the App regularly (this is especially important as promotional deals are often offered to consumers to increase their savings

5

Summing It All Up

You should have a pretty good understanding about how the wide world of web and digital technology impacts the couponer. As an active couponer myself, I have learned a few tips that are worth noting when it comes to shopping with coupons.

Tips to top off your savings with less stress:

1. Limit your internet site searching for coupons. (Too much time doesn't always equal bigger savings. Sometimes the opposite is true & more spending can occur.)

2. Don't download every app you come across. Try a few, but delete them if they don't meet your specific needs. Too many apps make for a cluttered phone.)

3. Update your apps when an update is available to keep your app functioning properly.

4. Shut off your phone periodically to speed up its response time when it's running slow.

5. Only print coupons for the items you plan on buying. (Cost goes up with excess paper & ink usage on unused coupons.)

6. Continue to balance out internet coupons with paper coupons. ("Out with the old & in with the new" is not always the best way. Too much dependency on the internet puts us at the mercy of technology which can fail.

7. Keep updated on store policies regarding ecoupons and the specific stores policy you shop at. Stores often will make changes to meet their specific needs.

8. Keep all your loyalty shopper cards on a separate keychain. With the increase in stores using these your car keys can become overwhelmed.

As technology advances we can expect the increase in online couponing, more coupon apps being released and the availability of more printable coupons. Does this mean an end to paper coupons? I doubt it. Statistically consumers like to feel their coupons and continue to participate in the experience of "old school couponing" for savings.

Couponing has come a long way since 1887 when it was first introduced to us by Coca Cola. Rumors are always circulating about the future of continued couponing due to frequent changes in store policies and procedures regarding them. However, we must keep one thing in mind manufacturers and retailers understand the shoppers search for a good deal and will continue to use this marketing tactic to compete with one another for our business.

As a wise consumer it is crucial to comparison shop for stretching that hard earned dollar. A coupon in hand doesn't always mean a deal in the buggy. Don't allow couponing to increase your spending, but rather decrease your debt by saving you money.

About the Author

Ann Haney has been an entrepreneur since 2001. She is the CEO of Aaron Publishing and founder of Ann Haney Ministries, author and publisher of 18 products including 5 year best seller "Homeschool Daily Planner for Curriculum." Four of Ann's 6 homeschooled children are entrepreneurs. She has conducted hundreds of motivational workshops around home schooling, successful entrepreneurship and raising entrepreneurs, couponing and more. In 2011 alone Ann presented 158 motivational workshops. She travels across the nation teaching people at Expos, Women Empowerment Workshops, Businesses, Networking Groups, Churches, UT Extension Offices, County Fairs, Government Facilities, Nonprofits, Schools and more how to become overcoming achievers as opposed to victims in today's society. Ann has been featured on Nashville Fox 17 news, Renee Bobb Talk Radio, Devin O'Day-Plain Jane Wisdom Talk Radio, Common $ense-The Money Show Talk Radio, in the Tennessean, Leaf Chronicle, DNJ, Shelbyville Times Gazette (where she was a weekly columnist in 2011), Illinois Alliant, Upside of Money "Faith & Finance", and The Nashville Examiner & Lebanon Democrat (where she is currently a columnist) She also appears live on up-towntalk.com in Murfreesboro, TN as a regular guest giving weekly tips & inspiration on couponing, budgeting and more. Her goal is helping people uncover their resources and team them up with their God-given potential to achieve success. Ann is the author of the book & corresponding financial empowerment workbook entitled, <u>Exploding Into Successful Entrepreneurship-Bringing Your God-Given Gift To The Surface For Success as well as her newest curriculum "Consumer Math Through Couponing."</u>

Ann has many organizational couponing materials to help the determined couponer find balance and success for their specific needs. Some of these products are as follows:

5   Part DVD teaching & Workbook "Changing Your Life Through Couponing"
      Consumer Math Through Couponing & Comparison Shopping Curriculum
      The Coupon Companion Handbook
      The Couponer's Guide to Drug Stores & More
      Numerous Couponing CD's including: 6 week startup, 7 steps to stockpiling success, shopping
            with small children, minimizing checkout challenges
      Binder Kit
      Shopping Templates
      Ultimate Guide to Stockpiling BONUS Freezer Guide
      Successful Couponing DVD
      Coupon Pouches
      The Complete Guide to Digital, Smart Phone & Online Coupons

For more information & to view these products or schedule Ann to speak at your event, business, church or school email Ann or visit:

www.annhaney.com
ann@annhaney.com

www.ingramcontent.com/pod-product-compliance
Lightning Source LLC
Chambersburg PA
CBHW051427200326
41520CB00023B/7386